ELLIE KNOWS BEST

ELLIE KNOWS BEST

Ellie Cady and Joan McWilliams

with illustrations by
Susan Mankamyer Sheets

Ellie Knows Best
by Ellie Cady and Joan McWilliams

Copyright © 2020 Ellie Cady and Joan McWilliams

Books may be purchased in quantity and/or for special sales by contacting the publisher or author through the website:
www.mcwilliamsmediation.com
    Email address: joan@mcwilliamsmediation.com
    Mailing Address: Joan McWilliams, Esq.
McWilliams Mediation Group LTD
PO Box 6216, Denver, CO 80206
Tel: (303) 830-0171
    Or, by contacting your local bookstore.

Cover Design: Susan Sheets and Nick Zelinger, NZ Graphics
Layout Design: Nick Zelinger, NZ Graphics
Editing: Jeanette Killip
Publisher: McWilliams Mediation Group LTD

ISBN: 978-1-7350243-0-1 (paperback)
ISBN: 978-1-7350243-1-8 (eBook)
Library of Congress Control Number: 2020911407

Printed in the United States of America

FIRST EDITION

1. Tween 2. Family & Relationships 3. Diaries 4. Tween Romance

Dedicated to our family
and to Watson and Rosie
(Woof Woof)

and to

Susan Sheets' mother, Martha Monnett,
an accomplished watercolor artist
who inspired others to find their inner artist
and never stop learning.

CONTENTS

Chapter 1   Middle School Frights 9

Chapter 2   Here We Go—The First Day . . 11

Chapter 3   New Friend/Old Friend 17

Chapter 4   Lunch Break 21

Chapter 5   Crush/Crushed 27

Chapter 6   Betrayal/Heartbreak 33

Chapter 7   Taking Risks 41

Chapter 8   Winter Break 49

Chapter 9   Always Ask 53

Chapter 10 Painful Situation 59

Chapter 11 New Friends/New Horizons . . 65

Chapter 12 One More Great Experience . . 71

Chapter 13 Lessons Learned 73

About the Authors and Illustrator 79

Bonus: Journal Pages 81

Chapter 1

Middle School Frights

Hi! I'm Ellie! I was about to go to Middle School, and I was scared to death. First of all, I heard there was a lot of homework. I already had a lot of homework in grade school, and I didn't know how I could do any more. Then, my best friend, Reese, told me that Middle School is really hard and that the teachers are mean. Besides that, I know there will be many more classes, and I don't know if I can keep them all organized.

After that, I heard that the older kids bully the younger kids, and I don't know what to do about it. I have a hard time with bullying. It really scares me because I can't predict how I should act when someone is being mean. In grade school, a friend of mine got bullied, and it really hurt her. Some of the other girls called her names and sent her really nasty texts. That put a lot of pressure on her because she felt like nobody liked her, and I don't want any of that in my life.

Thinking about Middle School sort of messed with my brain. I was worried all the time. I couldn't sleep and, actually, I didn't feel like eating. I tried not to tell my friends or my family because I didn't want them to think I was a wimp about going to a bigger school.

But, too bad. Ready or not. Here it comes—the first day of school!

Chapter 2

Here We Go—
The First Day

School started in August, and as soon as I stepped into the building, I froze in my tracks. I looked around, and I saw 7th and 8th graders who totally looked like they knew what they were doing. They were surrounded by friends and were laughing and joking. They were having a great time, and I was just petrified.

I knew I had to find my locker, and I knew it was in the sixth-grade hallway. I tried to look confident—like I knew what I was doing even though I didn't have a clue. Then, miracle of miracles, I looked down the hall, and there it was: Number 582. Success! I tried really hard to remember where it was located so I could find it next time without stressing. After that, it was pretty easy because it was next to an extra spot—kinda like a spare locker but not wide enough to make it another whole locker.

And then, my next challenge—I had to open the lock. This is another stresser. I turned the lock—one turn to the right to 10, one full turn to the left and back to the right to 15. Darn. One of my worst fears ... it didn't open. Whew, I hoped that nobody noticed.

OK. Don't panic. Try it again. Right then left then right. And amazing! When I turned the dial on the lock back to 15, it actually opened. Yay!

I reached into the locker and started to put my stuff away. One of my friends told me to put my backpack on the back hook to prevent my locker from jamming. I wouldn't want that to happen to me, so I hung my backpack on the hook just like my friend told me to do. Now I am ready to go to my first period class. What a relief.

When I turned around and started to go to class, I guess I was in my own little world because I didn't notice the confusion or how many people there were. When I looked down the hall, it gave me a little bit of anxiety. I just hadn't gotten used to the crowds and the noise. I remembered the single-file lines from grade school. But, this is middle school, and I was determined to love it (I hope).

I found my classroom and looked through the
doorway. I could see so many people, and they
were all standing in little groups of old friends.
It made me feel totally out of place. I didn't
have any "old friends," and I sure wish I knew
some of those people.

I slowly looked at the seating chart, and discovered that I sat in the front row (the best spot in my opinion) next to this boy named Logan. He seems really nice and a little cute. I definitely think that Reese will like him. I hope we can get to know each other and maybe even be good friends.

Wow, that's a really exciting way to start your first day of school. I found my locker, and I worked the lock combination. I found my math class, and I found my seat. I met Logan and hope we can be good friends. So fun!

Chapter 3

New Friend/Old Friend

I saw Reese in 3rd period, and I told her all about Logan. Even though I just met him, I felt like we got really close, in a weird but cool way. We had a chance to connect and exchange some ideas. He is cute, and I thought of him more as a friend. Hmmm—I don't know how he feels, but I would like to know him better.

Reese was excited to meet him. We decided to try and sit next to him at lunch if he didn't sit with his boy squad from his old school. We thought we would still sit there whether he was with them or not. Maybe we can make even more friends.

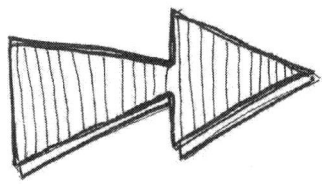

Third period was science. It was really exciting and fun. It was much more interesting than grade school. We took notes on photosynthesis (which I didn't really understand). Even though we just took notes, I got to sit next to Reese, and we talked alot about Logan and how dreamy he was. I told her how he flips his hair around like Justin Bieber, and that made us girls giggle a lot.

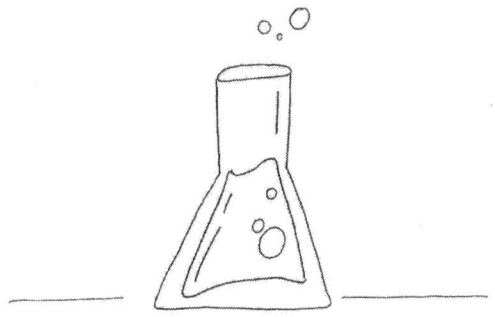

The bell rang, and we were off to 4th period— social studies. I wondered if I would ever get used to all of the people in the halls. It was so crowded and noisy—really different from grade school, but I'm starting to get used to it.

My social studies teacher was so nice. She told us that we would watch CNN10 everyday. It was so cool. One day, I saw our United States Senator on TV, and then later I met her in a restaurant. How neat.

I also really liked social studies because we got to choose our seats. I chose to sit next to Reese, and we slowly worked our way up the room to where Logan was sitting. I introduced Reese to Logan, and we sat down. He smiled and looked so cute. He probably thought we were really crazy because we kept getting closer and popping up everywhere. Reese started to blush, and she laughed nervously. I thought that was funny but a little strange (???????).

Chapter 4

Lunch Break

Reese and I weren't thinking (except we really were thinking), and we sat at one of the boy's squad tables for lunch. That's a table where all the boys crowd in to sit. Actually, (what a surprise), it was the table where Logan was sitting. The boys stared at us. We didn't understand that GIRLS were not allowed at the BOYS' table. It was embarrassing.

We jumped up, and after about 10 seconds as we were walking to another table, the whole cafeteria started laughing at us. We got uncomfortable and weirded out, we ran out and hid in the janitor's office.

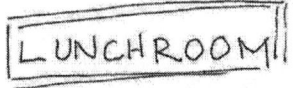

When we got in, there was this cold breeze coming out of the vent, and it gave us the chills. We ate our lunch as fast as we could so we could get out of that cold place.

As soon as the cafeteria opened the doors at the end of the lunch period, we made a run for it. Reese thinks nobody saw us, but she must have been delusional because everyone was staring at us and laughing.

How embarrassing—on the first day of school. And, worst of all, Logan saw us, but he wasn't laughing. He came over to us, and we were both so scared for what he was going to say. But, he ended up saying, "Don't worry about everyone laughing. It's not a big deal."

Logan turned around and walked outside to go throw his football with his friends. As soon as he got outside, everyone stopped laughing.

Reese said, "WOW! What a nice guy." That's what I thought too. He's nice AND he's cute.

Chapter 5

Crush/Crushed

At the end of the day, I was packing up my backpack and noticed Logan starting to approach me. He said, "Hi," and I said, "Hi" back. After that, Logan said, "I have a question." I answered, "Yes?" in a questioning voice. "Alright, here it goes," Logan says nervously. "Ellie, I've liked you ever since I met you in our first class, and I was wondering if you would be my girlfriend." "Of course! I'd love to be your girlfriend," I said. "Wait... what does that mean?" "Well," Logan said, "we can hang out more and go to the movies." "Oh that is so exciting," I exclaimed.

One thought that came to my mind after I said yes was WHO ASKS A GIRL TO BE THEIR GIRLFRIEND ON THE FIRST DAY OF MIDDLE SCHOOL, AND WHO SAYS "YES???!!!"

I couldn't wait to get home and call Reese to tell her my good news. I knew she would be so excited. But, I was wrong! I called her and told her my news: "Logan asked me to be his girlfriend!" There was a pause on the other end of the phone line. Reese wasn't excited. In fact, she just moaned and hung up. Wow ... I didn't expect that! That was rude. I guess, looking back, that Reese wanted Logan for her boyfriend. Live and learn! I wondered what would come next.

I was just hanging around at home on Saturday when my phone rang. I was hoping it was Logan, and, amazing surprise, it was!

"Hi Logan," I said with enthusiasm (I was really excited!). "Hi," he said. "Do you want to go see a movie at 2:00 later today?" "Oh, I would love to do that. Should we meet at the theater?" "Sounds good," said Logan. "Ok. See you later. Bye!"

I hung up the phone and shouted, "YIPEEEEEEE!"

I was really excited to go to the movies with Logan. I didn't really even care what we saw. It was my first date, and it was special.

I got dressed in my new yellow short dress and my black flats. It might have been a little too fancy, but I didn't care about that either. I was so excited. My mom took me to the theater.

I walked into the theater and looked around, but I didn't see Logan. I decided to call him. He answered his phone, and when I asked him where he was, he said, "Oh sorry, I had other plans and had to cancel."

I was shocked and sad, but I really wanted to see the movie. So, I bought a ticket and went inside. Who was sitting right in front of me? Logan and REESE! I couldn't believe it ... my best friend and my boyfriend are together to see the movie. "Wow, that hurts my feelings," I said out loud!

Logan turned around and saw me. He said, "Ellie? What are you doing here?" "Well," I said. "I came here because you asked me to go to the movies with you." Reese didn't even look at me or Logan. She put her head down. I guess she was worried about what I might say to her. Maybe she just didn't care.

Now, I'm mad and sad. I don't know what to say. I left the theater because I couldn't bear to watch them hanging out without me.

Chapter 6

Betrayal/ Heartbreak

This is an awful situation. Not only did Logan reject me, but Reese stopped talking to me. The pain of Logan's rejection was almost as bad as losing my best friend, Reese. They both hurt my feelings. I could hardly stand the thought of going to school on Monday when I would have to see them there. It makes me cry in pain.

I called my mom to ask her if she could come pick me up, and she asked why? I couldn't tell her what really happened so I just said, "The movie was cancelled."(It wasn't a complete lie because technically Logan did cancel the movie). My mom said to wait outside, and so I did.

What I wanted to do was to run away and hide.
I could hardly stand how bad this hurt. It made
me wonder if I had made a good choice of
friends. I met Logan on the first day of school.
I thought he was such a good person, but I guess
I was wrong. And Reese! I've known her since
kindergarten, and now I look back
and wonder if she was ever
a good influence.

When my mom picked me up, she knew something was wrong. She asked me again why the movie was cancelled. I couldn't hold it in anymore. I started to cry, and then I burst out the whole story. My mom listened. Then she stopped the car, got out, and opened my door. I got out, and she just hugged me and hugged me. It felt good to know that at least one person still liked me even if two people didn't.

I went home and went to my bedroom. I had never experienced pain like this, and I didn't know how to handle it. I cried and cried and cried until I just ran out of tears.

My mom came into my room and asked if I wanted to talk to someone about the situation. Someone like a counselor. I said, "Yes."

I knew what a counselor was. It's a person who talks to you about your feelings and any rough times you might be going through. This was definitely a rough time, so my mom made an appointment with a counselor who worked with kids. Her name was Mrs. Adams.

We went to the appointment, and it was pretty helpful. We talked about the situation, and Mrs Adams listened. She suggested that the next time I see Logan and Reese, I should tell them that they hurt my feelings, and then see how they react and then continue the conversation.

The next day I saw Logan in math. I was dreading to sit by him, but I knew I had to do it. I walked in and saw him twirling his pencil, and I said, "Hi Logan." He said, "Hi" back.

Then I said, "I want to talk to you about Saturday, it really hurt my feelings. I thought you were such a nice guy, but I guess you are a traitor."

Logan looked really surprised. I don't think he believed that I would have the nerve to say anything to him about the incident. And, I don't think he believed that I would have the guts to call him a traitor.

He sort of stammered around and finally said, "I'm sorry. I got in a bad situation because Reese asked me to go to the movie, and I didn't know how to handle it."

"Reese asked you?" I said in disbelief. "Yeah," he said. "Why didn't you just tell me, and we could have gone at a different time?" "Well," he said, I didn't want to hurt your feelings." "It hurt my feelings more to discover you and Reese at the theater then if we would have made different plans."

"By the way," I asked, "when did Reese ask you to go with her?" "Saturday morning," he said. "Wait, Logan, that's when you asked me, and I told Reese that you had asked me. She must have asked you after she knew that you had asked me. Boy...that is so bad. What a betrayal."

By the third period, I knew I would see Reese, and I was ready to confront her (just like the counselor said I should do). When I saw her, I went up to her and told her what Logan had said. Her face turned bright red like a hot pepper. She looked embarrassed. She knew she had been caught and that she had damaged our friendship. I really wondered if our relationship could be repaired. I thought to myself, "I don't think I could ever trust her again."

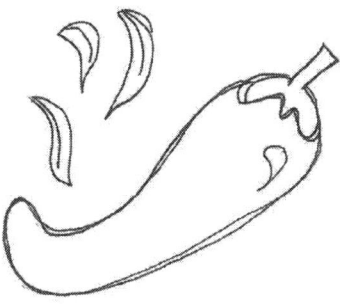

I was still in a lot of pain, but I had done what I needed to do. I had spoken my mind and made my position known. I had been honest with my friends even though they had not been honest with me. At least tonight, I can sleep knowing I did the right thing. Feels pretty darn good.

I found this quote by Trent Shelton on Google, and it's really fitting:

"Life has taught me that you can't control someone's loyalty. No matter how good you are to them, doesn't mean they'll treat you the same. No matter how much they mean to you, doesn't mean they'll value you the same. Sometimes the people you love the most, turn out to be the people you can trust the least."

It's just like what my mom has always told me, "You can't control what people do, but you can control how you react to them."

Chapter 7

Taking Risks

Since the Reese and Logan incident, I haven't had too many friends to hang out with, like go to the park or have sleepovers. I have been playing volleyball, but all of my teammates go to different schools. This isn't what I expected in middle school. Maybe it's a sign that I need to put away my hurt feelings and take bigger risks. Hmmmm ...

Hmmm.....

Once that idea came to my mind, it almost seemed to generate new friends. It was like it created an answer to my wishes. It's really weird, but other kids in my class started to come up to me and talk to me. Some of them invited me to sit with them at lunch. I liked having friends to sit with and chat because when I was alone and sitting by myself, I felt like I didn't fit in. It is crazy but when I wished for friends, they started to flood in.

This also made me think about my responsibility to my new friends. If they were being nice to me and including me in their activities, I needed to be nice to them. Now this may seem obvious, but I had to really think about it.

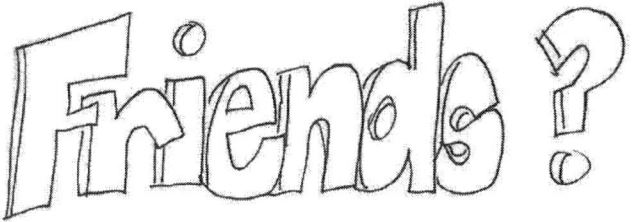

So, here's what I did. I started really making
an effort to talk to people. I asked some girls
to play volleyball at lunch. They seemed kind of
unsure because they hadn't played before, so
I taught them the basics, and they are getting
pretty good at it. Actually, we started to have a
really good time—laughing, giggling, and watching
some of the cuter boys (Oh yeah). A bunch of
us signed up for the volleyball team and took our
fun from the playground to the court.

I kept trying to branch out and think of other
things to do with new friends. One day, I saw a
girl, Kayla, and she looked sad. I asked her
what was wrong, and she said, "Nothing, it's
not important." That worried me. I ran home—
keeping my thoughts to myself.

I walked in the house and shouted for my mom.
Mom came to the living room and said, "Hi, honey.
How was your day?"

"It was good, I guess. I met a new girl named
Kayla, and she looked really sad. When I asked

her about it, she said that it wasn't important. and that made me worry. I didn't know if I should ask her more questions or just let the matter go."

My mom suggested that I ask Kayla to go on a bike ride, and maybe she would be more open to sharing her thoughts.

When I saw Kayla the next day, I asked her if she wanted to ride bikes after school. She really brightened up and said she would check with her mom.

She called me that afternoon, and we set a time for the next day. As it turned out, Kayla didn't live far from me, and we agreed to meet at a nearby park.

When we started riding, Kayla seemed much happier and was pleased to have me as a new friend. I was also pleased because that was one of my goals: make new friends.

I didn't know how to come up with the words to ask her why she was sad, so I just said, "You seemed sad yesterday, and I wondered if I could help."

Kayla said that she didn't like to talk about her problems, but it turned out that her great-grandma, who had just died, had given her a sea shell that connected the two of them. She used it to talk to her. But, she lost the shell when they moved to the neighborhood, and she is worried that she can't connect with her great-grandma anymore.

We talked for a long time, and I explained to her that she didn't need a shell to talk to her great-grandma. She could talk to her anytime.

Then I told Kayla about things she could do at school like helping in the office or helping with a special needs student. If she can help others, it might take her mind off of her problem.

Kayla was so pleased to have these suggestions. I was pleased because I had a new friend.

Kayla and I started getting together after school, and we had two sleepovers. It was fun, and all I had to do was start talking to her. We soon became good friends.

So, I learned a valuable lesson from my painful incident with Reese and Logan. To make friends, you have to be a friend.

Happy Day. School
was turning out to
be really good!

Chapter 8

Winter Break

I'm so excited that Winter Break is here so I can get a vacation from the Logan and Reese drama. I'm lucky because my family is going to California, and there is NO way I would see them there. I will get to spend time with my Grandma, my aunt and uncle, and my cousins, Riley and Cory. Yippee!

We have a great time together. We go boogie boarding, swimming and hiking together. Everybody loves each other, and I don't worry about much of anything. No drama. I basically just relax on the beach, and when I'm not boogie boarding, I search for sand dollars with my aunt.

My plane lands, and I am so excited to get my bags and go to the hotel so I can jump into my swimsuit and go into the water. We always try to get the room that looks out into the ocean and the beach so I can go by myself and still have someone watching me. It's so great—in the morning we can do whatever we want, and the next day we will go to Disneyland. My cousins always take me on the best rides

Even though I'm having a blast, sometimes Logan and Reese come to my mind. What a bummer ... I want to be rid of those thoughts. I better really try hard to focus on my vacation and how much fun I'm having with my cousins. It is the perfect remedy.

So ... on with the vacation ... what a treat!

Chapter 9

Always Ask

It's January. We returned to school from Winter Break, and I had made it through the first semester (amazing!). We began the day by starting a new unit in math. It was called number lines. We were basically learning how to solve problems using lines and going from the positive side to the negative side.

Everyone began to understand this new process except me. I just didn't quite get it. I didn't want to be that girl who asked a lot of questions, but I was getting lost.

Logan is in my class, and I think he understands the new math unit. I may need to ask him to explain it. Actually, that might help us to be friends again. When I think about it, Logan didn't mean to hurt me, he just went along with Reese. Even though that was a bad idea, it's ok to make mistakes, and I may have gotten a little too mad at him. Hmmm ... hope he can understand where I was coming from.

After school, I got my courage up and went over to where Logan was sitting. He wasn't exactly thrilled to see me coming. I kind of wanted to turn around and run away. But, I kept on going towards him, and I smiled.

"Hi, Logan," I said. He said, "Hi" back, but he was not enthusiastic. I think I understood that because the last time I had talked to him, I called him a traitor. Guess I better start out by apologizing. But actually, now that I think about it, I was waiting for him to apologize to me because he never really said he was sorry. Oh boy—who goes first?

I didn't know how to start, so I just said, "I'm sorry I called you a traitor. I was just hurt and angry." And then I said, "Looking back on the whole situation, I realized there was more to the problem than I knew right at that time."

There was an awkward silence moment because I was waiting for him to apologize to me. But, he never did. Darn!

I didn't know what to do, so I just asked him if he would help me with my math. Thank goodness, he said, "Yes."

WHEW !!

We started to work on the problems. Logan could really explain them in a way that I could understand them. I was so excited, and I told him that I really appreciated the help.

Then he said something that surprised me. "Ellie, I'm sorry that I didn't say anything before. Everytime I started to tell you that I was sorry, my friends were standing near me, and I was embarrassed. But, Ellie, I really am sorry. I'm not a traitor, and I feel bad that I did anything that would make you think that about me."

Wow! That made me feel so good. I can't exactly forget what happened, but Logan's apology made it a lot easier.

"Thank you, Logan," I said. "I really appreciate that. I hope we can be friends now." He agreed and said, "I would like that. Have you talked to Reese?" "No ... not yet, but I will."

I looked away as fast as I could because I didn't want to wreck the nice conversation I was having with Logan. I did think that I needed to talk to Reese about the situation and see how she feels. Boy, that will be uncomfortable. Darn. I didn't mean to get into that mess with her. I knew she still liked Logan, and I knew I had to talk to her. I worried that I might ruin my friendship with Logan and Reese forever.

Chapter 10

Painful Situation

Logan asked me if I would talk to Reese. I told him I would, but I didn't know what I would say to her. All I knew was that her betrayal broke my heart, and I could feel it all the way down to the middle of my heart.

I tried to come up with the words to speak, but all I could say was, "Cock-a-doodle-do!" "Cock-a-doodle-do?" What kind of language is that? I didn't think she would understand.

Geesh, I don't think I understand. I guess I must be REALLY nervous.

(That's me trying to deal with the pressure).

Ok—Ok! I'm going to get serious! I'm really worried because if I say one wrong thing, there goes the rest of our friendship right down the drain. As much as she hurt me, I still care about her, and I hope she doesn't misunderstand what I'm going to say.

At lunch, I decided I would text her. "Hi Reese." "Hi," she said back. "Do you want to meet up at the YogurtStand? I have some things on my mind." She said, "OK." "Does 4:15 work for you?" "Yes." "Great," I said. "See you later, Bye Bye."

Slam! The car door shut. I had my mom drop me off at the YogurtStand at 4:05 so I could prepare myself. I felt like I was practically shaking because I was so nervous. I didn't know if other people could see me shake, but I sure could feel it myself.

Ten minutes passed by really fast, and Reese showed up exactly at 4:15—right on time. Was that a good sign or a bad sign?

As she walked in, I noticed that she was really grumpy. Maybe she got up on the wrong side of the bed. Oh great! That was not a good sign.

As she sat down at my table, we decided to get some frozen yogurt. We went to the yogurt machine, and I got a salted caramel with a chocolate twist stick. Reese got strawberry yogurt in a bowl with mini peanut butter cups on top. We went back to the table, but neither of us said anything.

The silence was making me nervous. I think it was my turn to speak ... OK ... here I go. "Reese, we've never really talked about what happened with Logan. You were my best friend, and I trusted you. You really hurt me when you asked Logan to the movie. You knew that he asked me first, and you knew how excited I was."

"Well, I did know that Logan asked you first," said Reese. "I guess I was jealous because I liked him too."

I couldn't believe that she was so honest. I said,"Just because you were jealous doesn't mean you can hurt another person—especially your best friend." "Can I ever trust you again? I think not."

"I'm really sorry, Ellie. I don't know how to fix this. I'm still together with Logan, and I don't think we will break up just because we hurt you. All I can say is I'm sorry, and I promise that I won't betray you again."

I want to trust both of them again, but I am still deciding if I can do that.

Chapter 11

New Friends/
New Horizons

My friendship with Logan and Reese was still chilly. It was hard to rebuild trust, and, as I am learning, it takes a long time.

But I was ready to move on. I was already making some new friends, and I was looking forward to taking some new elective classes.

I walked into my first class, math, and the teacher announced that we had two new students, Birdie and Camden (Perfect timing, am I right?). To me, this meant that I might have two new friends. Hooray!

Wow! Birdie and Camden are twins, and they seem so nice. But I am aware of what might be coming, and I am a little cautious. It's hard to just blindly trust after you've been betrayed.

I picked a desk that was near their desks, and I introduced myself. They had just moved from California and seemed to be very smart.

As it turned out, they also had moved into a house that was down the street from my house (quite convenient).

When the cafeteria bell rang, I asked Birdie and Camden if they wanted to eat at my table. They were glad to have a place to go and said, "Yes." We went to the cafeteria together, and they seemed pleased to have the possibility of making a new friend. I know that I was pleased!

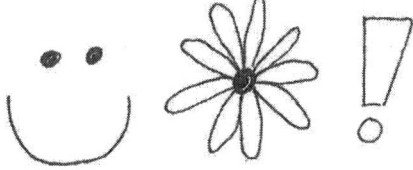

As luck would have it, we got along great. My cousins live in San Francisco, and that is where the twins lived before they moved. I had spent time there, so we had a lot to talk about like the cable cars, the beach, and the zoo. Their mom was a chef so they had great lunches. It was so much fun to connect with them.

We had something else in common. Birdie and I both LOVED volleyball. Camden was a soccer player, and he was very good. I used to play soccer but joined a volleyball team and found that it was a sport that I loved.

I took my volleyball outside with Birdie. She was extremely talented at bumping and setting the ball. She told me that she serves overhand, and her serve is like a bullet.

I had a brilliant idea. I asked her if she wanted to be on my volleyball team. I also asked her if she wanted to join the school volleyball club. She said "I'm going to need to talk to my mom about it, but that sounds really fun."

We walked home together, and I was excited to tell my mom about my new friends.

Chapter 12

One More Great Experience—At Last

My life was really picking up after my bad experience with Logan and Reese. Birdie and Camden were becoming good friends. Camden signed up for soccer and was playing on a 6th grade team. They played in a park near my house, and Birdie and I went to all the practices and the games that we could. Fun! Plus, it didn't hurt that Camden was sooooo cute!

Birdie and I tried out for volleyball, and we both got selected to be on a competitive team! Wow! Now we can really develop our skills.

I am definitely starting to treasure my friendship with Camden and Birdie. I just feel like I can trust them, and I know what it is to have friends you can't trust.

There are just some things that I know I really value. For example, if I tell Birdie that I want to tell her a secret, she will keep it confidential. If I make plans to get together with Camden and Birdie, they actually keep their commitment. They're both really good students, and that is important to me. Also, they are leaders. I can see that from the way they play volleyball and soccer and the way they participate in school. They both get good grades, and I think that is important.

I don't see Logan and Reese very much anymore. They are starting to be nicer again, but I still don't know if we can ever have that special connection. When your trust has been broken, it's hard to know if you can ever rely on them again. I can forgive them, but it's hard to forget what they have done; I will always remember that.

You probably guessed it by now—Camden is my new boyfriend (I think Logan is a little jealous). Camden and I made plans to go to the movies, and he actually showed up (I was very happy that he kept his promise). Birdie came too, and it was so much fun. My life is going great!

MOVIES

Chapter 13

Lessons Learned

Well, the school year has ended. I'm on my way to seventh grade, and that makes me really happy.

I learned a lot this year, in addition to my studies. I learned the things that I really appreciate. For example, when your feelings get hurt, you need to let it go, keep it in the past, and find new friends that you can trust. It's only in that way that you can start to heal. Change your attitude. That's a good way to solve these problems.

I also know now that I need to face my fears. It's uncomfortable, but when I face them it gets easier everyday. And, that is very true.

I will always ask my friends to be honest with me. It's just easier to stay really straight with each other.

It's good to have different groups of friends. It's nice to have a best friend, but you also need to have a bunch of different friends at school and out of school.

I really studied hard this year. I learned a lot and got good grades. My mom says that is really important, and I believe her. I can set my goals and follow through with them.

I learned to keep up with my schoolwork. It makes your life totally easier.

I ended up really liking my teachers, and I was always respectful of them. Teachers have a hard job, and it makes it easier if you are nice to them.

Like I said, I've really learned a lot this year. I went from being a scared kid on the first day to someone who solved a lot of problems during the year and really got my confidence back. It hasn't been without some pain. I experienced my share of pain. But, it was definitely worth it.

Seventh grade ...
I'm on my way!!! ... Can't wait!

About the Authors and Illustrator

Ellie Cady and **Joan McWilliams** are related! Ellie is Joan McWilliam's granddaughter. Joan and Ellie wrote this book while they were in quarantine due to the coronavirus. Ellie is in Middle School in Centennial, Colorado. She is going into 7th grade. Joan is an attorney/ mediator in Denver, Colorado.

Susan Mankamyer Sheets is a longtime friend of Ellie's Mom, Kendall Cady, and her Grandmother, Joan McWilliams. Susan illustrated this book during the 2020 Covid-19 quarantine. She is a Physical Education teacher in Douglas County Colorado.

—Bonus Section—
Journal Pages

My thoughts before 6th grade:

_____

_____

_____

_____

_____

_____

_____

_____

_____

What are my goals for 6th grade?

What do I look forward to in 6th grade?

What are my fears about 6th grade?

Who will I talk to if I feel uncomfortable?

_____

_____

_____

_____

_____

_____

_____

_____

_____

_____

_____

What will I take for lunch?

_____

_____

_____

_____

_____

_____

_____

_____

_____

_____

Who will I sit with in the lunchroom?

What will I wear on the first day of 6th grade?

_____

_____

_____

_____

_____

_____

_____

_____

_____

_____

_____

What will I take in my backpack?

_____

_____

_____

_____

_____

_____

_____

_____

_____

_____

Other thoughts and wishes?

_____

_____

_____

_____

_____

_____

_____

_____

_____

_____

Other thoughts and wishes?

Other thoughts and wishes?

My thoughts after 6th grade:

What were some of the best things about 6th grade?

What were some of the worst things about 6th grade?

Did I make any new friends?

What could I do differntly?

What are my plans for 7th grade?

_____

_____

_____

_____

_____

_____

_____

_____

_____

_____

_____

Other thoughts and wishes?

_____

_____

_____

_____

_____

_____

_____

_____

_____

_____

_____

Other thoughts and wishes?

Other thoughts and wishes?

Other thoughts and wishes?

_____

_____

_____

_____

_____

_____

_____

_____

_____

_____

_____

Other thoughts and wishes?

Other thoughts and wishes?

Made in the USA
Columbia, SC
04 September 2020